Librarian Tools

by Laura Hamilton Waxman

LERNER PUBLICATIONS ◆ MINNEAPOLIS

Note to Educators

Throughout this book, you'll find critical-thinking questions. These can be used to engage young readers in thinking critically about the topic and in using the text and photos to do so.

Lerner Publications Company
A division of Lerner Publishing Group, Inc.
241 First Avenue North
Minneapolis, MN 55401 USA

For reading levels and more information, look up this title at www.lernerbooks.com.

Main body text set in Helvetica Textbook Com Roman 23/49.
Typeface provided by Linotype AG.

Library of Congress Cataloging-in-Publication Data

Names: Waxman, Laura Hamilton, author.
Title: Librarian tools / Laura Hamilton Waxman.
Description: Minneapolis : Lerner Publications, [2020] | Series: Bumba Books. Community helpers tools of the trade | Includes bibliographical references and index.
Identifiers: LCCN 2018043339 (print) | LCCN 2018053620 (ebook) | ISBN 9781541556461 (eb pdf) | ISBN 9781541555617 (lb : alk. paper)
Subjects: LCSH: Library fittings and supplies—Juvenile literature. | Librarians—Juvenile literature.
Classification: LCC Z684 (ebook) | LCC Z684 .W35 2020 (print) | DDC 022/.9—dc23

LC record available at https://lccn.loc.gov/2018043339

Manufactured in the United States of America
1-46016-42933-11/6/2018

Table of Contents

Librarians

Librarians help people

at the library.

They use tools to do

their job.

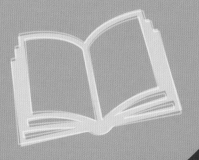

Librarians use computers.

They let librarians look up

things people want to learn.

Computers also show

the catalog.

It tells librarians where

books are in the library.

Librarians keep books

on shelves.

Shelves hold magazines

and newspapers too.

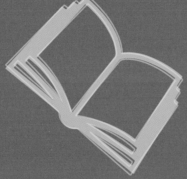

Sometimes librarians

need to move books.

They use a cart.

13

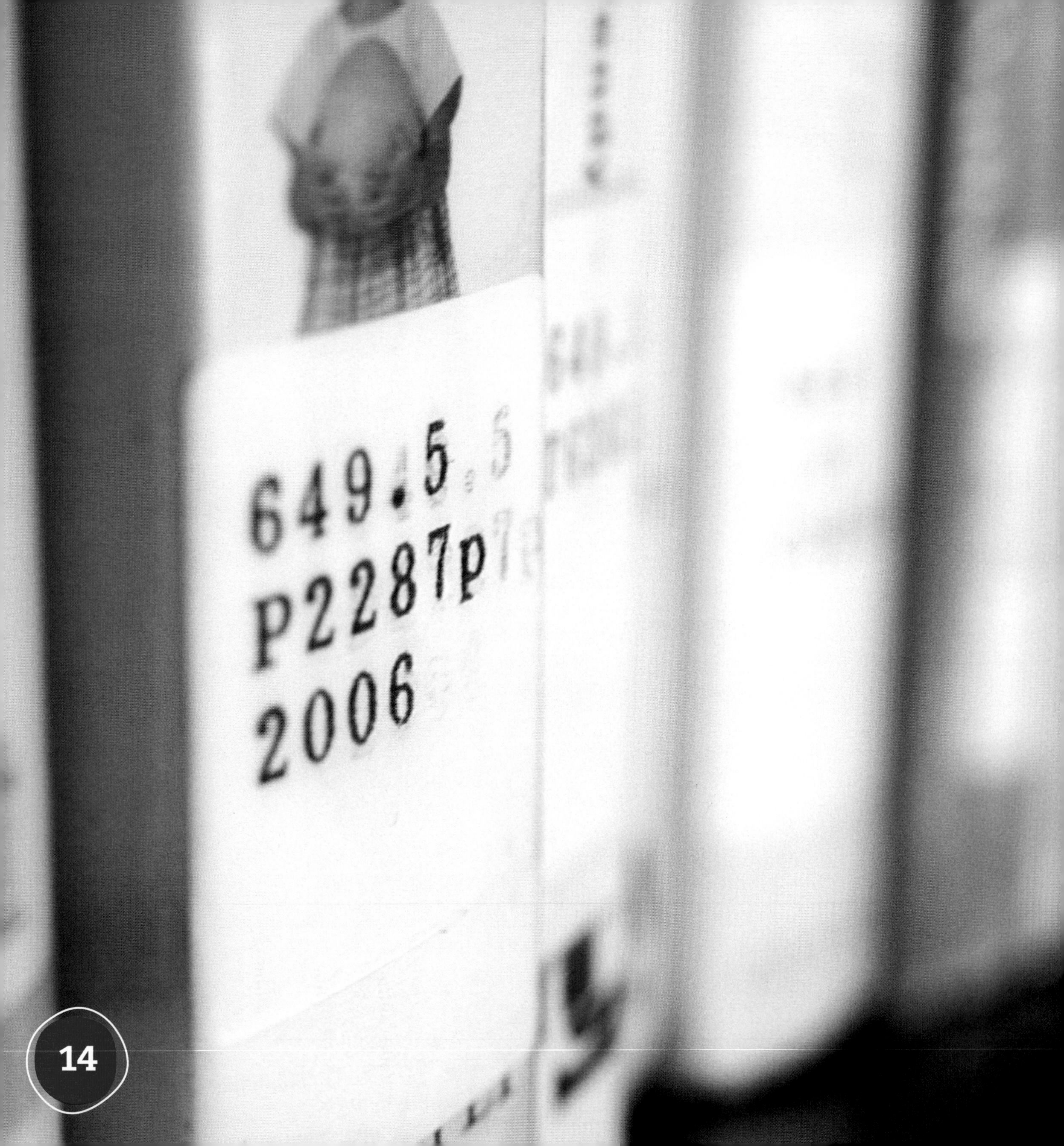
649.5
P2287p
2006

Librarians make sure each

book has a label.

It shows a book's call number.

A machine called a
book scanner checks
out books.

Do you know what
else you need to
check out a book?

It's important to be careful with library books.

But sometimes a book is harmed.

Special tape and glue can fix it.

Why do you think it's important to be careful with library books?

Some libraries have spaces

for making things.

Librarians help people use

the tools there.

Librarian Tools

cart

book labels

computer
catalog

shelves

Picture Glossary

book scanner

a machine that checks out library books

call number

the number that tells where a book belongs in a library

catalog

a list of all the books, movies, magazines, and newspapers in a library

harmed

hurt or damaged

23

Read More

Bellisario, Gina. *Librarians in My Community*. Minneapolis: Lerner Publications, 2019.

Clark, Rosalyn. *A Visit to the Library*. Minneapolis: Lerner Publications, 2018.

Siemens, Jared. *Librarians*. New York: AV2 by Weigl, 2016.

Index

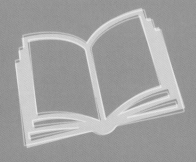

Photo Credits